Literacy Skills for
PAPUA NEW GUINEA

Improve your
WRITING
SKILLS

Susan Baing

OXFORD

OXFORD
UNIVERSITY PRESS
AUSTRALIA & NEW ZEALAND

253 Normanby Road, South Melbourne, Victoria 3205, Australia

Oxford University Press is a department of the University of Oxford.
It furthers the University's objective of excellence in research,
scholarship, and education by publishing worldwide in

Oxford New York

Auckland   Cape Town   Dar es Salaam   Hong Kong   Karachi
Kuala Lumpur   Madrid   Melbourne   Mexico City   Nairobi
New Delhi   Shanghai   Taipei   Toronto

With offices in

Argentina   Austria   Brazil   Chile   Czech Republic   France   Greece
Guatemala   Hungary   Italy   Japan   Poland   Portugal   Singapore
South Korea   Switzerland   Thailand   Turkey   Ukraine   Vietnam

OXFORD is a trademark of Oxford University Press
in the UK and in certain other countries

© Susan Baing 2002

First published 2002
Reprinted 2007, 2009, 2010, 2014, 2016 (D)

ISBN 978 0 19 551588 6.

Edited by Kate Deutrom and Paige Amor
Text and cover designed by Aileen Taylor
Illustrated by Melissa Webb
Typeset by Promptset Pty Ltd
Printed in Australia by Ligare Pty Ltd.

Contents

Overview   iv
Introduction to the student   1
Introduction to the teacher   2

Unit	Title	

1	An ordinary day	3
2	My diary for a week	6
3	Writing about my life—a journal	8
4	An autobiography—my life so far	10
5	A biography—the life of someone I know	12
6	A family activity	14
7	Independence Day	16
8	A special occasion	18
9	An exciting day	20
10	A story from my family	22
11	A story about the history of my area	24
12	Comparing my grandparent's life and my own life	26
13	Where I live—my environment	30
14	My favourite wild animal	32
15	A report on a school event	34
16	A personal letter	36
17	An invitation letter	38
18	A letter applying for a job	40
19	A letter asking for information	42
20	How staple food is prepared—a process	44
21	A recipe	46
22	How to make something	48
23	How to get somewhere	51
24	Rules of a game	54
25	How to write an advertisement	56
26	Giving your personal opinion	58
27	Giving reasons and explanations for your opinion	60
28	Writing speech	64
29	Write a traditional story	66
30	Writing a story based on a legend	68
31	Writing an imaginary story	70
32	Write a play—a legend or story we have read	72
33	Write a play based on something in your life	74

Overview—Improve Your Writing Skills

Introduction to the student
Unit 1   An ordinary day
Unit 2   My diary for a week
Unit 3   Writing about my life—a journal
Unit 4   An autobiography—my life so far
Unit 5   A biography—the life of someone I know
Unit 6   A family activity
Unit 7   Independence Day
Unit 8   A special occasion
Unit 9   An exciting day
Unit 10   A story from my family
Unit 11   A story about the history of my area
Unit 12   Comparing my grandparent's life and my own life
Unit 13   Where I live—my environment
Unit 14   My favourite wild animal
Unit 15   A report on a school event
Unit 16   A personal letter
Unit 17   An invitation letter
Unit 18   A letter applying for a job
Unit 19   A letter asking for information
Unit 20   How staple food is prepared
Unit 21   A recipe
Unit 22   How to make something
Unit 23   How to get somewhere
Unit 24   Rules of a game
Unit 25   How to write an advertisement
Unit 26   Giving your personal opinion
Unit 27   Giving reasons and explanations for your opinion
Unit 28   Writing speech
Unit 29   Write a traditional story
Unit 30   Writing a story based on a legend
Unit 31   Writing an imaginary story
Unit 32   Write a play—a legend or story we have read
Unit 33   Write a play based on something in your life

Please use your Oxford University Press Dictionary when required.
Answer all questions in your exercise book.

To the student

This book will show you some ways you can improve your writing skills. Each unit in the book tells you what you need to know to do different kinds of writing.

You will learn how to write descriptions, reports, diaries, journals, instructions, biographies and autobiographies, historical stories, comparisons, letters, directions, rules, advertisements, opinions, legends, imaginary stories and plays. You can use the skills in this book every time you do any one of these kinds of writing.

1   There are instructions for you to follow.

2   There is an example of the kind of writing. (Sometimes the example isn't finished.)

3   There are some ideas for you do to get ready to write.

4   There is a list of steps you take to get you started on your writing.

5   There is a list of words that you can use when you do your writing.

Here are some ideas to help you do the units.

1   Talk about each kind of writing in your class. Your teacher will tell you how to do this.

2   Your teacher will help you to share your ideas by brainstorming with your class. This means you give the teacher lots of ideas from your group to put on the blackboard.

3   When you can see a lot of ideas, you can choose the ideas you want to use. Then you use these ideas to make a plan about your writing.

4   Use the plan to write the first try at your writing. This is called a *draft*. Sometimes you need to write more than one draft.

5   Read your writing carefully and make sure there are no mistakes.

6   When you are sure your writing is ready, write a good copy of your writing for other people to read.

To the teacher

The units in this book demonstrate the elements of different kinds of writing. Students are shown a standardised approach to any writing task, as well as the different requirements of different kinds of writing tasks. Some suggestions are given about the practice of the skills, but you will be able to provide many more opportunities for them to practice the skills.

The examples provided are not usually complete, but are given to demonstrate some of the styles of writing. Students could be first asked to complete the story, and then to write their own similar story.

The word lists provided are also restricted. Encourage the students, through class competition and displays, to add relevant words to the lists, and to use the listed words and their own words when they write.

Unit 1

An ordinary day

Often we do the same things most days, in the same way and at the same time. We call these our habits or routines.

Examples: *I eat kaukau for breakfast everyday.*
Every school day morning I walk to school.
I go to church at eight o'clock every Sunday.

Fill in this table. Write what you do every school day.

Daily Routine

Time of day	What I do

Now use the ideas you have written on your table. Describe a day in your life to someone who does not know you. Write about what happens on an ordinary school day. Start with the first things you do in the morning. Finish with the last things you do before you go to sleep at night.

Make your story interesting by putting in the small things that happen in your day. Put the things you do during the day in the order they happen. Use these words that show order: *then, after, next, later.*

Example:

My school days

Most of my school days are the same.

My mother wakes me up at six o'clock. I go outside onto my veranda and look at what kind of day it is. Then, I collect some firewood from under the house. Next, I make the fire. My mother brings some water in a kettle and she makes tea for me. I eat some cold bananas from the night before. After eating, I go and have a wash. While I wash, my mother cooks some scones for me to take to school.

Next, I pick up my school bag. Inside are my homework and my scones for lunch. I say goodbye to my mother at about half past seven, and then I walk through the gardens and get onto the road. Later, I meet up with my friends and we walk together. Usually, someone has a funny story to tell about what happened at the weekend.

When we arrive at school ...

Now you try

Getting ready

Make your own list of things that are important in your day. Here are some things you could write about:

- what time you usually get up in the morning

- what you usually do before school each day

- what time you usually leave the house or dormitory

- how you usually get to school and what you see on your way

- what you usually do when you get to the classroom area

- how your day usually goes

- what time you usually go back to your house or dormitory

- what you usually do after you get home

- what time you usually go to bed.

Steps

1 Give your story a title.

2 Begin by writing something about the title.

3 Say: Who? What? Where? When?

4 Write what happens in order.

5 Finish by writing what you feel about your day.

6 Use the present tense for your verbs (go, walk, stop).

Look back at the example story and see if you can find these ideas. Put a line under all the verbs. Are they in the present tense?

Here are some words you could use in your story

during	at six o'clock	in the garden
first	at midday	in a hurry
first of all	in the afternoon	in a minute
a long way	at night	in time for (something)
on time	early	usually
on foot	late	after breakfast
by bus	everyday	after lunch
by canoe	on Mondays	after school
across the road	the bridge	the river

My diary for a week

A diary is a notebook where you write down what happens each day. A diary is written for you yourself to read. You don't usually read someone else's diary. You can use a diary for two things:
To *plan* the things you are going to do each day
To write down or *record* what you did each day.

Example:

Monday	New school term starts (plan) I saw my uncle at school. (record)
Tuesday	Buy some pens (plan)
Wednesday	Mum gave me a new book. (record)
Thursday	Youth Group at Church (plan)
Friday	Helped my grandfather in the garden after school (record)
Saturday	Go with Dad to get new clothes (plan)
Sunday	Church (plan) Saw Jack in the afternoon, walked up to the main road together (record)

Now you try

Write a diary of your own life. Write the diary for two weeks.

Getting ready

Make a table like the table above. Make the table for two weeks. Write in what your plans are for the next two weeks.

- What are you going to do each day?

- If you do not have a plan for a day, leave the space.

- Use present tense verbs for making a plan.

- Use past tense verbs for writing a record.

You can use a diary to write longer pieces of writing.

Example:

> At 7 o'clock, I got out of bed and dressed, ready to go on the truck with my father. He was taking me into the town to buy some new clothes for school. We left the village on the truck at 7:30 am. The truck journey took just over an hour. We went to a clothing shop and my father got me two pairs of shorts and three shirts. We went home on the truck at 3:30 pm.

Now you try

Write a paragraph about what you did one day this week.

Getting ready

- make a list of all the things you did in one day

- write about the people you did these things with

- keep the list in the order that you did the things

- record the time you did each thing

- use *I* or *we* when you are recording the events

- use the past tense

Here are some words you could use

during the morning ...	at last	from 4:00 pm until 6:00 pm
went to ... to get ...	after that	last Sunday
did not get back from ...	later	for one hour
until one o'clock	earlier	for a few minutes
by nine o'clock	finally	since the weekend

3

Writing about my life— a journal

A journal is like a diary. But you write different things in a journal. You write your plans and a record of facts in a diary. But in a journal, you write more about how you think and feel about what happened that day as well.

Example:

Monday: It was the first day of school. I was not happy getting out of bed this morning. The holidays have been fun. I have really enjoyed helping my grandfather getting his new garden ready. It is a special garden planted after the death of my grandmother. We have worked together each day, and he has told me a lot about the history of my clan. I know he will miss me today. It will be Friday before I can help him again, and then, only after school.

Wednesday: Mum gave me a new book today. She got it when she went to town with the Women's Group. Mum is very kind to me. She knows how much I want to do well at school and helps me whenever she can.

Friday: At last Friday has come. How long the week has seemed. My grandfather did a lot of planting while I was at school. As soon as I got home, I rushed to the garden. Grandfather was happy to see me. He showed me the new work and then we talked about what we can do next. I feel pleased to be doing this with him.

Sunday: I had a real surprise today—Jack came to visit. It is a year since he left the village and he had lots of stories to tell. We walked together up to the main road and talked a lot. I feel that Jack is doing the right thing with his life and I hope that I can do the same things when I finish school. He spends a lot of time with his grandfather too, when he can get back to the village.

Write a journal for two weeks. You should have a least five entries in your journal.

Getting ready

Here are some things you could write about:

- use the diary you have written for the past two weeks

- pick diary entries that record things you have feelings about

- write how you feel about those events

- use *I* or *we*

- use the past tense to talk about what happened: *Mum gave me a new book today.*

- use the future tense to talk about things that have not happened yet: *It will be Friday before I can help him.*

- use the present tense to talk about things that are still happening: *Mum is very kind to me.*

Here are some words you could use

Only a dream …	I wish	angry
That's what I would like …	I hope	sad
I can't wait …	I want	pleased
It is my idea that …	I believe	unhappy
It seems to me …	My dream	hoping

Unit *4*

An autobiography—my life so far

An *autobiography* tells about the important things that have happened to you. It is the story of your life, written by you.

Example:

My life so far

My life has not been very long yet, but a lot of things have happened to me.

I am the youngest in my family. I was born thirteen years ago in a village called Ragiampun, Morobe Province. I still live in this village with my family. I was very small when I was born and my aunties, who helped my mother, did not think I would live. But one aunty took me down to the river and washed me, and I began to cry. I was named Capera, after this aunty.

I got sick a lot and I grew very slowly at first. When I was three years old I got malaria badly and my parents had to take me to the hospital in Lae. I remember being carried on my father's back to catch the PMV. Luckily, I got better. Later, I got pneumonia, but this time I went to the Aid Post. I still get a lot of colds.

When I was very young, I played with all my cousins in the village. We liked to play near the river. When I turned six, my parents enrolled me at our elementary school. The school is here in my village, only a short walk from my house. At school I ...

Now you try

Write the story of your life so far.

Getting ready

Make your own list of things that are important in your life story.
Here are some things you could write about:

- where and when you were born

- what names your parents gave you

- what your position is in your family (eldest etc)

- who your older and younger brothers and sisters are

- what things you can remember

- what games you played

- when and where you started school

Steps

1 Give your story a title.

2 Begin by writing something about the title.

3 Say: Who? What? Where? When?

4 Write what happens in order.

5 Finish by writing what you feel about your life so far.

6 Write in the past tense, because everything you write about
   has already happened.

Here are some words you could use

at that time	aid post	oldest	was born
many years ago	church	youngest	grew fast
a good time	hospital	in the middle	grew slowly
a bad time	illness	our family	got sick
first name	sore	exciting games	got better
namesake	ulcer	began school	was strong
my dog	cough	an earthquake	was weak

A biography—the life of someone I know

A *biography* tells about important events that have happened in a person's life. Some biographies are written about famous people. But you can also write a biography about someone you know.

Example:

My grandmother, Mumi

I have decided to write about my grandmother, Mumi, because she is an important old woman in our village.

My grandmother does not know when she was born, but she knows that she was a young girl when the Second World War came to Papua New Guinea. So, she was probably born about 1935. When she was a child, she stayed in the village and learnt about looking after the garden and cooking food.

She remembers an important feast that was held every year. This was the Christmas Feast. The Lutheran Missionaries made a bird called a dove out of wood and my grandmother remembers seeing the dove go down a long rope from a high tower to the ground. She joined in the dancing that the women do at this feast.

My grandmother remembers the first planes that flew over our village. In 1940, a plane landed on the beach. She was very frightened at that time.

During the war, my great-grandfather took the family to live in the mountains near our village. They stayed in hiding until 1945. One day my grandmother said that Australian soldiers came along the track from the coast. She had not seen any white people except missionaries before. The soldiers were very sick and tired and grandmother helped look after them until they left.

Write the biography of someone who is very old. This could be a member of the family, or someone who lives near you. You will need to talk to the person to find out about their life.

Getting ready

Make a list of the things that are important in the old person's life. Here are some things you could write about:

- who the old person is and how old they are

- where they were born and where they live now

- what they did in the past including important events

- how you know the person

- why you have chosen this particular person.

Steps

1 Give your story a title.
2 Begin by writing something about the title.
3 Write what happens in order.
4 Finish by writing what you feel about the person's life.
5 Write in the past tense.

Here are some words you could use

family friend	custom	tribal fight	proud of
tutul	leader	bride-price	admire
ancestor	patrol	mission	convert
priest	kiap	interesting	prevent

A family activity

What are some of the things your family does together? The family activity could be a gardening activity, making something or a social activity.

Example:

Banana growing

Bananas are an important food in the place where I live. Our family grows a lot of bananas. There are many kinds of bananas, but they are all grown using the same method.

Making a banana garden is something the family does together. First, we all go to an old banana garden to find banana suckers. These are the small banana plants that grow at the bottom of the old plants, which we have already cut down. The women dig up the suckers and carry them to a new garden, while the men clear the place for the new banana plants to be planted. Both men and women work at keeping the growing bananas plants clear of weeds. Any children who are old enough also do the weeding. We all go to the garden every two weeks.

When the banana fruit starts to get quite big, the young boys climb up the stem using a pole ladder. They take old, dry banana leaves up the ladder to the fruit, and wrap the fruit in the old banana leaves.

Later, both men and women cut down the banana plant to harvest the fruit when we need to eat them.

Now you try

Make a list of some family activities. Now pick one activity to write a story about.

Getting ready

Make a list of the things that are important about the family activity. Here are some things you could write about:

- what kind of activity have you chosen?

- who does the activity?

- are there any parts of the activity done by special people?

- how long does the activity take?

- what is the result of the activity?

Steps

1   Give your story a title, and explain a little bit about the title.

2   Explain any words or ideas that could be new to your reader.

3   Write about the activity in the order that it happens.

4   Write about who does the different parts of the activity.

5   Write what the result of the activity is.

Here are some words you could use

food crop	plant	work together
cash crop	weed	side by side
plant	get ripe	join in
fish trap	harvest	special job
sago	chop down	only the boys
kaukau	build	the women's job
making salt	cooperate	hard work
hunting	enjoy	sharing the work

Independence Day

Independence Day in Papua New Guinea is celebrated in many different ways. What did your family do last Independence Day?

Example:

My Independence Day

Every Independence Day I can remember has been different. Last year was different too.

Last Independence Day it was raining! We had been preparing to perform our dances at the celebrations for six weeks. When I woke up and saw the rain, I nearly cried. I knew that if the rain went on, we could not wear our feather headdresses. They have been passed down in our family for many years, and my grandfather is very careful about looking after them.

I ate my breakfast under the house so I could see if the rain had stopped. About eight o'clock, I saw some blue sky over the mountains. I watched for a while and then ran to tell my parents. We packed up my costume for the dance, and soon set off for the school grounds. My grandfather carried the headdress.

When we reached the school, I could see all my friends being dressed by their parents. We went to join them. Next, my parents helped me get ready. Grandfather put the feathers on my head. Then, the headmaster blew a whistle and we all ...

Now you try

Write about what happened to you and your family on Independence Day. Write in the *past tense* and use *time words* and other words that tell the order things happened in.

Getting ready

Make a list of things that were important about the day, and how you celebrated it. Here are some things you could write about:

- what was different or the same about last Independence Day

- what the weather was like

- who you were with and where you went for the celebration

- what you wore

- what happened during the day

- how you felt when the day was over.

Steps

1 Give your story a title.
2 Begin by writing something about the title.
3 Say: Who? What? Where? When?
4 Write about what happens in order.
5 Finish by writing with what you felt about the day.

Here are some words you could use

every year	all day	in the centre	felt proud
during September	a band	as a result	beating drums
at that time	a crowd	welcome	performed
the week before	the flag	choirs	thirsty
at sunset	the oval	coconuts	tired
the National anthem	flowers	stalls	happy
dancing groups	a speech	soft drinks	dusty

A special occasion

There are some days in our communities that are special because something different and exciting happens.

Example:

Opening of the new women's centre

The women in our village wanted a building where they could meet and learn about new skills. They wrote to our Member of Parliament and he sent some money. The women also did some fund-raising by selling food at the market. It took six weeks for the new building to be built. Then it was time to have a celebration.

This was a special occasion, because we do not often have new buildings like this one. It was made of sawn wood, and had a tin roof. There was even a water tank to catch the rainwater. Everyone in the village took part in the celebration. The men had helped to put the building up. Some of my uncles are expert carpenters, and my father knows how to make cement.

The day started early. At dawn, my mother and aunties went to get kaukau from a special garden. I went with my cousins to get plenty of water, and then we went and picked lots of fern leaves and ibika. My brothers chopped a large pile of firewood. Everyone was busy. The food was soon cooking over the fires.

By ten o'clock we had finished our preparations, so we sat down to wait for the Member of Parliament to arrive. It was my job to put a string of flowers around his neck. I felt very nervous ...

Write about what happened on a special day in your community.

Getting ready

Think about some special occasions, such as a bride–price celebration, harvest feast, or opening of a new church or school. Here are some things you could write about:

- when the celebration is held and how often it happens

- how long it lasts

- who takes part in it and what your community does

- what you did and what you saw at the celebration

- what you felt at the celebration.

Steps

1 Give your story a title.

2 Begin by writing something about the title.

3 Write about what you saw on the day. (*Who? What? Where? When?*)

4 Write in the past tense (*took, helped, started*).

5 Use time words to tell when things happened (*then, after that*)

6 Finish by writing what you felt about the day.

Here are some words you could use

for two weeks	all day	table	noisy
through the village	all week	tablecloth	cheerful
under the trees	an hour	plate	cheering
bowls of food	money	banana leaf	feel tired
a string band	collection	plastic	patient
thanksgiving	shady	money pole	painted

An exciting day

Write a true story about a time you had an adventure or did something exciting.

Example:

Picnic at the hot water pools

I never thought I would save someone from drowning, but that is what I did the day we went for a picnic to the hot water pools.

The picnic happened during the wet season. My cousins and I had got bored with sitting around the house and we decided to go for a long walk, even though it was raining. We set off through the kunai grass towards the river. The path was very muddy, and we slipped around a lot. As we got near the river, the rain stopped, but it was still cold. We thought how good it would be to sit for a while in the hot water.

We needed to cross the river to get to the hot pools. The river was flooding its banks. We cut down some old banana plants. We used the trunks to help the youngest children float across the river. Some of them were not good swimmers. Then we set off.

At first, everything went well. However, near the opposite bank of the river was a place where the water swirled around. One of my youngest cousins got caught in the water going round and round. His hands started to slip off the slippery banana. I was the closest too him, but too far away to grab him. I saw him get pulled under the water, so I swam quickly across the current to hold him. By the time I reached the place, he had disappeared under the water. I shouted to my sister to bring over her banana trunk. Then I dived under the muddy water. It was hard to see anything, but then I caught sight of my cousin floating …

Think of some times when you have done something exciting.

Getting ready

Here are some things you could write about:

- when the event took place

- who went with you

- where you went and why you went to that place

- what happened when you got there.

Steps

1 Start your story with a sentence to make your reader want to keep reading. You want the reader to think, 'What happened next?' Write *I never thought I would ever save someone from drowning* rather than, *At the weekend, I had an adventure.*

2 Remember to use words that tell about time and order such as: *first, then, soon, after, before, next, while, at last.*

Here are some words you could use

the morning	beside	through	happy
the afternoon	near	over	favourite
the bush	between	across	sudden
the weekend	opposite	under	afraid
an accident	a long way	during	brave
the beach	a short way	by mistake	ready

A story from my family

Most families have a story about the family that everyone in the family knows.

Example:

The catfish story

Every time my grandmother gets sick, she blames it on something that happened when she was a girl. We have heard this story so many times that it has a name. We call it the catfish story.

As you can guess, the story has something to do with catfish. Near our village, there are some little streams with deep pools and that is where the catfish live. Catfish have whiskers on their faces and some sharp spikes on their backs. They are good to eat, so the women in the village like to go and catch them.

One day my grandmother was fishing for catfish with the other girls. They used nets made of woven string, like a bilum, on a circle of bamboo. They went to the place where they knew there were a lot of catfish. My grandmother was wading in a muddy part of the pool when she stepped on something sharp. She called out that she had stepped on a catfish, but went on with the fishing.

Later, when she was sitting down at the edge of the stream, she noticed that her foot was bleeding. When she was walking home with the girls, she started to feel sick.

After that, whenever she got sick, my grandmother would blame the catfish, and she would tell the story again. It did not matter what kind of sickness she had, she still blamed it on the catfish, even when she was quite old.

Write a family story that everyone knows.

Getting ready

Think of some stories that are told in your family. Here are some things you could write about:

- when and where the story took place

- who the story is about and what happened in the story

- why your story is told in your family.

Steps

1 Give your story a title.
2 Begin by writing something about the title.
3 Say: Who? What? Where? When?
4 Tell the story in the order that it happened.
5 Finish by writing why the story is important for your family.

Here are some words you could use

aunty	at first	swamp	favourite
uncle	after that	river	similar
cousin	then	mountain	different
sister	next	reef	following
brother	later	beach	every week
grandmother	finally	mangroves	often
grandfather	the result	forest	sometimes
friends	led to	waterfall	never

A story about the history of my area

The history of your area goes back as long as people have lived there. Find out about a true story from your area's history and write the story.

Example:

The last canoe voyage

The villagers along the Huon coast near Lae use to sail large canoes with two masts. These canoes were called *casal*. The canoes were carved out of tree trunks and had sails of woven pandanus. The canoes were used to trade with Lae and other villages and sometimes long, dangerous journeys were made.

The canoes have not been used since the 1950s. At that time, three canoes left Voco Point in Lae to go home to their villages of Uki and Sycoma. When they were halfway home, there was a very bad storm. The sea was very rough. The canoes tried to reach the shore, but two of the canoes sank.

The people on the third canoe held onto their boat, which was almost all under the water. There was a mother and a baby on this canoe. The mother saved her baby by putting him in a bilum and putting the bilum up the mast, which was sticking out of the water.

The people stayed on their canoe until the sea became calmer. Then they were rescued by people from a nearby village. After this, people along the Huon Coast decided not to travel to Lae by sea.

Now you try

Write a true story about the history of your area.

Getting ready

Ask some old people to tell you some stories about the history of your area. The stories could be about trade, voyages, exchanges, when white people came, when the church came, or when cash crops started. Here are some things you could write about:

- when the story took place

- where the story took place

- who the story is about

- what happened in the story.

Steps

1 Give your story a title.

2 Write a little bit about the title.

3 Write about what happened in time order.

4 Use the past tense.

5 Finish by writing why the story is important.

Here are some words you could use

important	until now	after that	kina shells
custom	until then	as a result	clay pots
culture	these days	this led to	travelled
tradition	in those days	lost	surprised
change	kiap	different	unexpected
happen	tutul	similar	new
continue	Christianity	trade route	frightening
used to be	before then	stone axes	thought

Comparing my grandparents' life and my own life

Papua New Guinea is very different today from when your grandparents were young. Write a story comparing your own life with the life of one of your grandparents when they were young. You should write about some things that are different, and some things that are the same.

Example:

How life has changed—my grandfather's life compared with my own life

Papua New Guinea has changed very much in the last fifty years. Our country today is a very different place from when my grandfather was growing up.

My grandfather was born at the end of the Second World War (1945). He is not sure of the year. I was born in 1990. I know when I was born because of my health clinic book. We were both born in our village, near Tambul in the Western Highlands.

When my grandfather was young, Papua New Guinea was looked after by Australia. He told me that there was a kiap at Tambul. The kiap was an Australian man. The kiap was the boss of the whole district. He would come and get men to take them to work on the plantations. My grandfather said his own father went to work in Rabaul for many years. When I was a child, Papua New Guinea was already an independent country. This means the country is looked after by people who are elected.

Everyday was very hard work for my grandfather's family. At that time, there was no trade store in our area. They had to grow all their food. My grandfather remembers having to help his mother feed the pigs, and go with her to make the kaukau gardens. Nowadays, in our village we have some trade stores but my parents still grow a lot of our food, and my mother still looks after pigs.

Both my grandfather and I had plenty of time to play games when we were young. My grandfather played ... I played ...

In my grandfather's time, everybody lived in a house made of bush material ... However, in my time, our house is made of ...

My grandfather used to wear ... However, today, I wear ...

Pig exchanges were important when my grandfather was young. They are still important today. In my grandfather's time ... Now ...

My grandfather did not go to school because ... I am lucky because now we have a school in my village. I can go up to Grade 8 in my school ...

You can see that some things about the way we live in my area have not changed. My grandfather has seen a lot of changes but because we live in a village, many things have stayed the same. It would be different if we lived in a town.

Now you try

Write about the life of one of your grandparents, compared to your own life.

Getting ready

Here are some things you could talk about:

- when your grandparent was young

- what was happening in PNG at that time

- what your grandparent's daily life was like

- where they lived, what they wore, what they ate

- how they were educated

- what special events they took part in

- now do all the same points for your own life.

Steps

1 Decide who you are going to write about.

2 Make a list of the points you want to write about.

3 Talk to your grandparent, or someone who knew your grandparent when they were young.

4 Ask them about the points on your list.

5 Draw up a plan for your story like this. (There are other things you could write about too):

My grandparent's life	My life
When he/she was born	When I was born
Where he/she was born	Where I was born
What games he/she played when he/she was very young	What games I played when I was very young
How he/she was educated	How I am being educated
The kind of house he/she had	The kind of house I live in
The clothes he/she wore	The clothes I wear
The food he/she ate	The food I eat

6 Give your story a title.

7 Write a short paragraph about the title.

8 Write about each point in turn. Write about your grandparent, and then write about yourself.

9 Then go on and do the same for the next point on your list.

10 Write a last paragraph, which shows how alike or how different your lives are.

Here are some words you could use

aeroplane	carved	carve
arrows	colourful	cut
axe blades	(un)comfortable	die
bride-price	customary	educate
bird of paradise	dangerous	exchange
cash-crop	forgotten	explore
cassowaries	forested	fight
Christianity	grassy	gather
clan	peaceful	hunt
conch-shells	religious	eave
development	simple	put the roof on
drums	valuable	put clay paints on
gold	violent	own (a design)
government	woven	keep (a custom)
language	travel by	believe in
men's house	in contrast with	convert (to Christianity)
patrol	different from	be educated at/by
trade-routes	similar to	give up (tribal fighting)
tradition	compared to	a better way

Where I live—my environment

Your environment consists of all the things that are around you. If you live in a town, your environment will be different to that of a student who lives in a village. When writing about the environment, we paint a word picture for the reader, so that he/she can see in their minds what the place is like.

Example:

My environment

I live in a wide river valley, not far from the northern coast of Papua New Guinea. The river is important in my environment.

My house is near the bank of the river. The house is just above a sandy beach. The house is made of bush materials, such as tree trunks and palm leaves. The roof is made of dried grass put on in thick layers to keep the rain out.

Around my house is a small flower garden. Behind the house is a small building with no sides where we sit sometimes. This is built around a tree, and has bougainvillea plants growing over it. There is a platform for my family to sit on. We often eat our food there ...

Now you try

Write a description of your environment.

Getting ready

Here are some things you could talk about:

• what the buildings are made of

- where it is (in a town, near a river)

- what is close to the house and what is further away

- what you can see on the horizon (where the land or sea meets the sky)

- what your garden, village or neighbourhood is like.

Steps

1 Give your writing a title.

2 Write a little bit about the title.

3 First, write about the part of your environment that is close to you and then about what is further away.

4 Use the present tense.

5 Use words that tell about place.

6 Use descriptive words.

7 Finish by describing your feelings about your environment.

Here are some words you could use

between ... and ...	in front of	coconut	muddy
right before my eyes	at the front	group	mountains
the first thing I see	behind	path	hills
in the distance	beside	grassy	ocean
at the top of the hill	ahead	large	highway
on the riverbank	opposite	level	city roads
in the middle	along	steep	busy
further back	set among	square	noisy
to the left of	close to the centre	stony	dusty
at one side of	water pump	straight	dry
surrounded by	bamboo	sandy	

My favourite wild animal

An *information report* describes a thing or animal. It gives facts about that thing or animal. What is your favourite wild animal?

Example:

Ants—my favourite wild animal

Ants are insects with six legs. There are many different kinds of ants, with different colours, sizes and habitats. However, all ants have some things about them that are the same, such as their body parts, and how they act together in groups.

All ants have bodies that are divided into parts. Their hard skeletons are outside their bodies. All ants have heads, front parts of the body (called thoraxes) and back parts (called abdomens). Ants have six jointed legs, two eyes, two feelers (antennae) on their heads, and strong jaws.

Ants live together in large nests. They all work together looking after the whole nest. Only one ant is the queen. She lays all the eggs for the whole nest. She is looked after by worker ants. The worker ants can carry up to eight times their own weight.

Ants find their way by light patterns, by special sense organs in the joints of their legs, and by chemical paths they leave between the nest and where they find food.

Now you try

Write a report about your favourite animal. You can also draw a diagram to show important things about the animal.

Getting ready

Here are some things you could talk about:

- what your favourite wild animal is and why you have chosen it

- which country it is found in and what its habitat is like (where it lives)

- what it looks like and how it behaves

- what it feeds on

- whether humans use the animal in any way

- any special points, such as whether or not it is in danger of extinction.

Steps

1 Write a title for your report.
2 Tell some important things about the animal first.
3 Repeat the topic name often in your report.
4 Use paragraphs to organise the facts.
5 Use the present tense (are, climbs, lives) and action verbs.

Here are some words you could use

bird	Goura pigeon	sea-horse	powerful
bones	habitat	seaweed	alert
burrow cheetah	height	stripes	carry
claws	hornbill leopard	spots	chew
coral	mangrove	tail	breed
dolphin	nesting habits	teeth	avoid
elephant	panda	web	capture
environment	paws	strong	compete
feathers	reef	friendly	crawl
fur	sand-dune	valuable	eat

A report on a school event

A report is about something that has already happened. Write a report about an interesting event or an accident.

Example:

Fund raising day

Our school needed some new books for the library. The teachers and parents decided to have a fund-raising day to get some money to buy books.

First, they had some meetings to decide what kinds of things the school could do to raise money. They decided to have a Fun Day on the school oval, with games and competitions and stalls selling food and things the students had made. They then decided on a date.

All week the students had been getting things ready. We had mowed the grass and made some bush material stalls for people to use for selling things. We had set up some dartboards and some arrow targets. On Saturday, the 17th of March, we arrived early at school. Then we helped the teachers fix up the drinks stall and put ropes around the dancing area.

After that a lot of people came. I went to help ...

Now you try

Write about something that happened at school.

Getting ready

Think about some of the things that happen at school. Here are some ideas that will help you write the report:

• give the date and time of the event

- give the exact place where it happened

- what you did—were you taking part in the event, or watching something happen

- who was involved in the event, who organised the event

- how the event started

- what the most important or exciting things that happened were

- how the event ended

- what your feelings were about the event.

Steps

1 Give your report a title.

2 First tell the reader what you are writing about—the topic.

3 Then, arrange all the events in the order that they happened.

4 Join the events with words that help your reader make sense of what you have written.

5 Use simple past tense verbs (*he ran*), past continuous verbs (*he was running*), or past perfect (*had been running*).

Here are some words you could use

sports day	happy	during	rice-balls
school grounds	laughter	the stage	hot dogs
were working	tried	speeches	soft drinks
in the middle of	noisy	prizes	scones
in between	tent	races	hungry
until 5 o'clock	early	choir	plenty

16

A personal letter

You write personal letters for many different reasons. You could write to ask someone to help you buy something, or to tell someone about something important that happened.

Example:

Box 4241
Wewak
ESP

31 October 2003

Dear Bro

How are you? I hope you are well.

I'm writing to tell you that our mother is sick. She has had a bad cold for many weeks now, and the medicine the doctor gave her isn't working.

I think you should come home and see her. She keeps asking for you.

Mum hasn't been able to go to the garden and she doesn't want to eat banana now. She says it hurts her teeth. Please send some money through the Post Office so we can buy her some rice.

Hope to see you soon.

Your sister

Sera

Now you try

Write a personal letter to a friend or family member.

Getting ready

Here are some things you could talk about:

- give some news

- say thank you for something

- ask for something

- say you are sorry about something

- write special greetings, such as for a birthday or Christmas.

Steps

1 Put your address and the date at the top of the letter.

3 Greet the person you are writing to. It is usual to put *Dear* and then their name.

4 Use *I* when you are writing.

5 Use everyday language, such as when you speak to a person.

6 End the letter with some closing words, for example: *Love from your son, See you soon, Remember to write, Best wishes.*

7 Put your address on the back of the envelope.

Here are some words you could use

pass my hello	remember	need	some money
I am well	forget	expect	some clothes
hope to hear	unlucky	miss	next month
sends her love	family	wait	a baby
favourite	at present	receive	the funeral
at the weekend	telephone	send	prepare
yesterday	funny	post	at home

An invitation letter

Write a letter to your cousin. Ask him/her to come and stay with you in the town or village at some time in the future. Tell them exactly how to get to where you are living, and make arrangements for meeting them.

Example:

Box 474
Waigani Post Office
NCD

3 November 2003

Dear Rebecca

I would like you to come and stay with me for Christmas. You could come when school finishes, and go back in time for when school starts.

You can come on one of the PMVs that come to Port Moresby everyday from Rigo. When you reply to this letter, tell me the day you are coming and I'll make sure I'm at the bus stop to meet you. But just in case I miss you, this is how to get to my house ...

There are lots of things you will like doing in the town ...

Please bring some coconuts with you—they are so expensive here ...

Write as soon as you can to tell me that you are coming. It'll be fun!

Love from your sister

Tina

Write an invitation letter to your cousin.

Getting ready

Here are some things you could write in the letter:

- when they should come and how they should travel

- where to meet you and what to do if you are not there

- what you plan to do while they visit you

- when they should leave to go back home

- what arrangements they should make for going home

- what they should bring with them

- ask them to write and say they are coming.

Steps

1   Follow the same steps as for the personal letter in Unit 16.

2   Put in all the information that your friend or cousin needs.

Here are some words you could use

a bag	a long drive	your toothbrush	arrive
a bus	a short walk	Parliament	return
bus fare	some ibika	a dance	stay
bus stop	some bananas	my Church	sleep
market	television	big supermarket	ask for
a towel	museum	take a bus	wait for
your shoes	problems	get off at	look for
fresh fish	the beach	spend a few days	prefer
not far from	turn left	look around for	choose
in three days	go straight	after a month	buy

A letter applying for a job

You have seen an advertisement for some jobs in a new company. Write a formal letter to the company and apply for one of the jobs.

Example:

Box 474
Waigani
NCD

23 September 2003

The Personnel Manager
Super Special Supermarket
Box 1113
Boroko

Dear Sir or Madam

**Subject: Application for the job of
Checkout Assistant**

I wish to apply for the job of Checkout Assistant advertised in the Post Courier, 21 September 2003.

I am seventeen years old. I finished Grade 10 at Gordons High School last year. I enclose a copy of my Grade 10 certificate.

I enclose references from the pastor at my church and from the headmaster of Gordons High School.

My telephone number is 325673. I am able to come for an interview at any time.

Yours faithfully

Jennifer Tau

Write a letter applying for a job.

Getting ready

Here are the points you need to write about:

• the job you are interested in and where you saw it advertised

• your name, age and address

• details of your education

• the names of some people who can give a report on you.

Steps

1 Set out the letter like the example—you need to put the address of the company, as well as your own address, plus the date.

2 If you don't know the name of the person you are writing to, put *Dear Sir* or *Dear Madam*.

3 Write what job you are applying for.

4 Write your age and about your education.

5 Give the names of references.

6 Finish by saying if you are able to go to an interview.

7 End the letter with *Yours faithfully* if you started with *Dear Sir*, or *Yours sincerely* if you started with a person's name.

Here are some words you could use

grades	above average	look forward to
honest	careful	work hard
results	helpful	hope that
office	polite	write in answer to
reply	my education	part-time work
duties	get along well with	headmaster

A letter asking for information

Sometimes you need to write and ask for materials to use in a project, or to find out information. This kind of letter needs to be very clear, so people know what you want.

Example:

Box 474
Waigani
NCD

15 May 2003

Mr Peter Barter
Manager
Madang Resort Hotel

Dear Mr Barter

I am a student at Pari Primary School. I am doing a project on tourism in Madang. I would like you to send me some brochures about your hotel, especially some with pictures in them. I will use these to show how people enjoy themselves in Madang.

Could you please post the brochures to my post box address.

Thank you very much for your help.

Yours sincerely

Rebecca Tau

Now you try

Write to an office or organisation asking them to send you something.

Getting ready

Here are some ideas to help you.

- find out who you can write to—a Government Department, a Non-Government Organisation (NGO), an Embassy from another country, a company

- write a clear address for them to send the things to

- state clearly what material/information you need

- say what you are going to do with the material/information

- say how the material/information should be sent to you

- thank the organisation.

Steps

1 Decide what you want to ask for and what you need it for.

2 Set out the letter like the example.

Here are some words you could use

recipes	some information	famous	cost
education	(your) country	interesting	describe
farming	my postal address	modern	discuss
customs	my special interest	some photos	know
games	my school	some maps	learn
history	my class	popular	like
music	my youth group	send to	get
prices	a guide to	hope that	study
religion	interested in	by post	

How staple food is prepared——a process

When you write about a process, you describe the steps you go through to do or make something.

Example:

How to cook bananas

The people of the Markham Valley grow many kinds of bananas that they use for food. They grow bananas all year, but sometimes, if there is a drought, the bananas will not grow so well. They need good soil and a warm climate to grow well.

Women harvest the bananas. They use a bush knife to cut down the banana plant. They also use a woven strap to thread through the bunch of bananas so that they can carry them home on their heads.

When they get to the village, the women break the banana bunch up into small bunches. They sit on the ground. They have clay pots nearby. They line the clay pot with ibika leaves. They light a fire with wood.

The women take off the banana skins with a bone tool. They fill the pot to the top with bananas and then put in some water. They cover the pot with some folded banana leaves and put an empty half coconut shell on top. They put the pot onto the wood fire. After a while, when they see that the bananas are mostly cooked, they squeeze some coconut milk on top.

Now you try

Write the steps you go through to prepare your staple food.

Getting ready

Here are some ideas you need to think about:

- what the staple food is and the special time or season for it

- is there a special place to grow the food

- who goes to get the food and what tools are needed

- what steps are taken to get the food ready to eat and how long does it take to prepare.

Steps

1 Give your process a title.

2 Write about where it grows.

3 Write the steps you go through in order.

4 Use action verbs. Use the present tense.

Here are some words you could use

above sea level	ditches	yam
fresh-water swamp	drains	these days
near the beach	mounds	in between
near the forest	grater	dig
near the river	spade	press
there are several steps	hillside	scrape
in the past we	mountain	peel
used to trade for	slope	wash
a special season for	level ground	collect
so that	bamboo tube	dry
after the (rain, dry season, flood)	wrapping	

A recipe

A recipe is a list of steps to cook some food. This is a kind of process. There is a special way of setting out a recipe.

Example:

Baked fish with bananas

Ingredients

1 fresh fish
10 cooking bananas
4 ripe tomatoes
six banana leaves

2 bunches of spring onions
a piece of ginger root
a scraped coconut

Method

1. Make the fire for baking, by letting the coals form.
2. Clean and scale the fish.
3. Put the bananas in the fire to cook.
4. Wash the onions and tomatoes.
5. Chop them into small pieces.
6. Scrape the skin off the ginger and chop it finely.
7. Lay the fish on some softened banana leaves.
8. Put all the other ingredients on it.
9. Squeeze the coconut milk over it.
10. Wrap up the parcel and bake on the fire.
11. Serve on more banana leaves with the baked bananas.

Now you try

Write a recipe for something you know how to cook.

Getting ready

Here are some ideas to help you write your recipe:

- what are the ingredients or things you need for the recipe

- do you need any special tools to do the cooking

- what are the steps you take

- do you need to warn the person about anything, for example, *Take care when chopping the chillies*

- do you need to give any instructions about serving the food?

Steps

1 Give your recipe a title.
2 Make a list of the ingredients and any tools you need.
3 Put the steps you take in order (method).
4 Give any warning directions you need.
5 Write how to serve the food.

Here are some words you could use

baking dish	piece	golden brown	clean
bowl	pot	the first step	combine
flour	salt	add the ... and ...	cool
fruit	saucepan	stir to dissolve	chop
grater	skin	beat well	fresh
grease	slice	oil	hot
heat	spoon	lumpy	warm
juice	stove	frequently	smooth
moisture	sugar	taste	softened

22

How to make something

A set of steps to make something, or do something are called *instructions*. There are three parts to instructions:
The aim of the instruction (this can be the title).
What things you need to follow the instructions (ingredients).
The steps you take to follow the instructions.

Example:

Making a clay pot in the Markham valley

Things you need
Some clay and water
A wooden paddle (about the size of a spoon)
Something sharp such as a hair comb
A ring (20 cm across made of cane)
Firewood

Steps
1. Go to the bush near the village and get the clay. (This is usually done by women.)
2. Beat the clay with the paddle to make sure it is smooth.
3. Roll the clay into long thin pieces. (This step and the following steps are usually done by men.)
4. Make the pot base by coiling the clay into a flat circle.
5. Now build up the side of the pot with coils. Use the water to make the coils stick together. Use the cane ring to keep the pot upright.
6. Smooth out the coils with water and the wooden paddle.
7. Make a lip on the pot so it can be carried to and from the fire.
8. Use the sharp comb or tool to make designs on the pot.

9. Leave the pot to dry for about three weeks.
10. Make a big pile of firewood and put the dry pot on top.
11. Light the fire and leave the pot there for one hour.
12. Seal the inside of the pot by boiling ripe bananas in it.

We can also show how to make something by drawing a flow-chart:

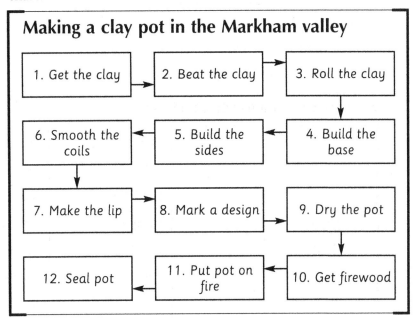

Making a clay pot in the Markham valley

1. Get the clay → 2. Beat the clay → 3. Roll the clay

6. Smooth the coils ← 5. Build the sides ← 4. Build the base

7. Make the lip → 8. Mark a design → 9. Dry the pot

12. Seal pot ← 11. Put pot on fire ← 10. Get firewood

Now you try

Write a set of instructions to show someone how to make something.

Getting ready

Here are some ideas to help you write your instructions:

- write about something you know how to make or something you know how to use (a toy, a traditional tool, a bilum)

- try to make or do the thing first, so that you make sure you get the steps in order

Steps

1 Give your instructions a title that tells what you are doing.

2 Write a list of anything you need.

3 Put the steps in the order that you need to do them.

4 Use instruction words (turn, fold, cut).

5 Give exact details (2 cm long).

6 Use the present tense.

7 Use time-linking words such as *Start*, *Now*.

8 Draw diagrams to help someone make the thing.

Here are some words you could use

first get a	look for	shells
earlier	gather	coconuts
later	hunt for	leaves
meanwhile	scrape	bamboo
after that	smooth	feathers
the next stage	carve	paper
the last thing to do	poke	scissors
burn some coconut shells	collect	a knife
don't forget to	pick up	string
be careful of	divide into two	glue
fold the paper into two	light a fire	a pencil
on the opposite side/edge	boil some leaves	a pen
in the middle of	paint the design	a ruler
talk to an old person about	ask for help	colours
put it aside to dry/set	about half of	shapes

How to get somewhere

Directions are a list of steps you would take to get from one place to another. Sometimes we need to write directions telling someone how to get somewhere.

Example:

> ## How to get from the school to my house
>
> When you leave the school gate, turn to the right and walk along the road towards the school for 100 metres. There you will find a small path that is on the left. Where the path joins the road there is a large mango tree.
>
> Turn into the small path. Walk towards the hills. The path runs past some peanut and corn gardens. After ten minutes you will come to a small river. Cross the river on the rope bridge. On the other side is the main road. You need to be careful now, as many big trucks use this road. Cross the road and walk along the left-hand side for 50 metres. There you will see a small trade-store belonging to my uncle. Look out for the sign that says Mutrus Tobacco on the roof.
>
> There is a track leading from the main road, just before you reach the bridge. The signpost says Lus Ples. Go along the track and up a small hill. Near the top of the hill there is a group of houses. My house is the one that is on the right, in between the casuarinas trees. I will be waiting under the house.

Map of the way to my house

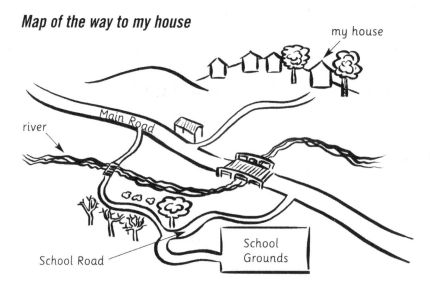

Now you try

Write a set of directions describing how a friend can get from the school to your house. It is very important that you write clear directions or else your friend might go to the wrong house! Here are some points that will help you:

Getting ready

Here are some ideas to help you write your directions:

- how far away is your house from the school?

- how long will the journey take?

- does your friend need to use public transport to get to your house, or will they be able to walk?

- what is the first thing they should do after leaving the school?

- what are the next steps?

- are there any special places or things they need to look out for?

- where will you be when they arrive?

Steps

1   Draw a small map. Put the school, the roads, rivers, paths and your house on the map.

2   Use the map to write the steps your friend would take to get from the school to your house.

3   Make sure the steps are in order.

4   Use instruction words such as *cross, turn, take.*

5   Use prepositions such as *to, from.*

Here are some words you could use

basketball court	beach	when you get to
community school	bridge	arrive at
a kilometre	bus stop	belonging to
mango tree	by canoe	cross the river
market	corner	look for
minutes	ditch	get off (the bus)
roadworks	gate	wait at (the bus stop)
roundabout	high school	above
supermarket	an hour	after
sports ground	path	along
street sign	river	around
traffic lights	road	behind
trade store	rocky	between
the distance is	rough	into
it will take you	stony	near
the first turn on the left	steep	opposite
the second turn	shady	outside
look out for	short	past
be careful of	wide	towards
on foot	dusty	underneath
the path runs past	main (street)	as well as

Rules of a game

Our ancestors had games that they played as children. Some of these games have been forgotten but some are still played today. We need to have a set of rules to play a game, so that the game is played the same way each time (unless you want to change it!) and so that the people feel that the game is played fairly.

Example:

Hipitoi game

My grandmother taught me how to play this hand game. The game was played to teach children how to make quick hand and eye movements that were needed during tribal fights.

Two children play the game at once. The child who starts the game is the leader.

There are four-hand movements—left thumb up, right thumb up, both thumbs up, no thumbs up. The leader calls 'hipitoi' and both children make a movement at the same time.

If both children make different movements, it is the second child's turn to start the game. If both children make the same movement, whoever calls 'hipitoi ra' first wins a point, and it is their turn to lead off the next round.

The game ends when the children have had enough. The child with the most points is the winner.

Now you try

Write instructions for a game you know.

Getting ready

Here are some ideas to help you write your rules:

- what is the game called?

- how do you know about it?

- how many people can play, and do you need any equipment?

- what are the rules, and where do you need to be?

- do you have to say anything?

- how does the game start and end, and how do you know who is the winner?

Steps

1 Write the title of the game and why it is played, if you know.

3 Write how many people play the game.

4 Write the steps to show how the game is played.

5 Write how the game finishes and who wins.

Here are some words you could use

running	a bat	your hands/feet	catch
sand	a bow	your eyes	climb
stones	a catch	some shells	pass
skills	a circle	some string	throw
swimming	a pair	favourite	win
water	a partner	at the end	popular
weapons	a player	show someone	circle
winner	a runner	at the same time	square
an arrow	a stick	during	tired
a ball	a target	finally	interesting

How to write an advertisement

Advertising is a kind of writing that is used when you try to get someone to buy something.

Example:

Visit the beautiful town of Goroka

Goroka is the entrance to the amazing Highlands of Papua New Guinea.

Stay at the Bird of Paradise Hotel and experience Paradise yourself!

Visit our Coffee Plantations and see how coffee is grown and processed.

See the strange and exciting Mud-Men of Asaro.

Come for the Goroka Show and see the fantastic cultures of Papua New Guinea.

Take home some of the beautiful hand-made baskets and bags from our craft markets.

Now you try

Write an advertisement in which you are trying to get tourists to visit Papua New Guinea.

Getting ready

Here are some ideas to help you write your advertisement:

- write the name of the place and say how to get there

- write some of the things people might like to see or do

- write where visitors can stay during there visit

- write what they can take home to remind them of their visit (artefacts or souvenirs).

Steps

1   Write the name of the place at the start of your advertisement.

2   Write about the things people could see or do using colourful words.

3   Use strong adjectives (the most beautiful …)

Here are some words you could use

adventure	nature	peaceful	bring (a friend)
animals	ocean	smiling	buy carvings
beach	orchids	special	climb
gardens	reef	tropical	come (soon)
coral	village life	wonderful	discover
culture	welcome	travel	dive
fish	adventurous	crocodiles	explore
guest-house	friendly	birds	visit
flowers	happy	towns	watch fish
island	historical	markets	watch dolphins
pool	natural	traditional	watch dances

Giving your personal opinion

Sometimes, you want to tell other people what you think about something. This is your *personal opinion*. Opinions are what you think about things. For example: *I think that was a good story. I think soccer is the best game.* When you write about your opinions you use words like *I think*, or *I believe.*

Example:

Dear Editor

I think that the council needs to make some improve-ments to the market. If the council did this, I believe people would be happier to go there and sell their food. Now the market is too crowded and the sellers have no room to put their food out. Also, there is a lot of rubbish and water lying around. There are no proper places for people to display their food and I think this is unhealthy.

I believe there are some things the council could do to make the market better. They could make benches so that the food is not laid out on the ground. They could put rubbish bins there and collect the rubbish. They could dig drains so that the water goes away.

Now you try

Write a letter to the newspaper giving your personal opinion about people selling food and other things in the street, or along a highway. Make some suggestions and say why you think the suggestions are good ideas.

Getting ready

Here are some ideas to help you write your letter:

- decide if you think street selling is good or bad

- think of some reasons why street selling is good or bad

- say what you think could make street selling better, and give reasons for your ideas.

Steps

1 Write the topic of your letter.

2 Write clearly what your opinion about the topic is and give your reasons.

3 Write some facts to help people believe your opinion.

4 Write what can be done and say why that should be done.

Here are some words you could use

healthy	women	coconuts	laws
unhealthy	men	cash	policemen
dirty	young boys	shops	cars
criminals	gambling	buying	guns
smoking	thieves	selling	stealing
cigarettes	no space	crowding	throwing
betel nut	markets	walking	newspapers
second-hand clothes	peanuts	driving	tables
fences	lamb flaps	running	sacks
danger	cooking	crossing	on the ground
dangerous	fires	laughing	dusty
accident	cards	talking	diseases
pedestrians	pawpaw	playing	move (to)
children	kaukau	spitting	

Giving reasons and explanations for your opinion

When you want someone to believe your opinion you need to give reasons and explanations. You need to write facts. Facts are things that can be proved. Facts are true. For example: *Port Moresby is the biggest city in Papua New Guinea. There are coffee plantations near Goroka.*

Try this

Write if these sentences are facts or opinions.

1 I think Leo is stupid.

2 The House of Parliament is in Port Moresby.

3 Lae is in Morobe.

4 I think it will rain tomorrow.

5 My mother cooks me scones each morning.

6 My grandfather is dead.

7 I believe I will get a good mark in the test.

8 Selling food in the street is bad.

9 The people living in settlements are all thieves.

10 Port Moresby has a dry season and a wet season.

Now read the following example of a piece of writing that gives reasons and explanations about an opinion.

Example

Are our children getting the right kind of food?

Everyday, outside our school, you can see a row of women sitting and selling food through the fence to the school children. Often, this food is not good for the children because it will not help them grow up strong and healthy. We need to teach children and parents about eating good foods. On the other hand, some of the school children think it is all right to eat things like cheesepops and iceblocks. However, if we want our country to be healthy, we need to have children who are healthy.

Papua New Guinea has the highest rate of malnutrition in the Pacific. There is no reason why the rate should be so high. Our country can grow enough good food for everybody. It has fertile soil, a good growing climate and a lot of water. But many children do not eat the right kind of food. The right kind of food is food that helps the body grow and stay healthy, such as kaukau and green vegetables.

Babies are sometimes not fed enough. Young children need to be fed five or six times a day. When they finish being breast fed, they need to eat lots of food that helps them grow. They need to eat some oil everyday, and have some fruit, starchy food, meat or eggs, as well as milk.

Some parents give their children lamb-flaps. This meat has a lot of fat in it, which is not good for our health. Instead, they should give their children rice and tinned fish, because this food is better for the body.

I do not think that our children are eating the right kinds of food. I think that our government needs to do more to help parents learn how to feed their children properly. The children can learn more about good foods at school. The school can make sure that only good foods are sold near the school. The government needs to help the farmers grow the right kind of food to help keep children healthy, so that every child can grow up strong and healthy.

Answer these questions about the previous passage.

1   What is the writer's opinion about how many children are fed?

2   What does the writer say some children think?

3   What is the first reason and explanation that the writer gives?

4   Why does the writer say we should not have malnutrition?

5   What is the second reason and explanation that the writer gives?

6   What is the third reason and explanation that the writer gives?

7   What does the writer say to finish the writing?

Write your opinion about tourists coming to Papua New Guinea. You should write about what you think, and give reasons and explanations. You should write some facts as well as your opinion.

Getting ready

Here are some ideas to help you write.

• decide if you are for or against tourism in Papua New Guinea

• write a list of the reasons for your opinion

• find some facts you can use as your explanation

• think of some examples of tourism you could use

Steps

1   Write your first paragraph to introduce your opinion.

2   Write in the introduction what some other people think. This is a different opinion from your opinion.

3   Write two or three paragraphs that will help your reader agree with your opinion.

4   Use some facts and some examples to make your writing stronger.

5   Finish your writing by saying what you think will help the problem get solved.

6   Use *being* verbs (is, was, are).

7   Use thinking and feeling words (I feel, I'd like)

8   Use linking words to make it easy for the reader to understand your opinion (so, but, on the other hand).

Here are some words you could use

in addition	agree	carefully	firstly
compared with	disagree	personal	secondly
this led to	argue	accept	thirdly
point of view	prove	allow	finally
a lot of	fact	appear	many
take these steps	numbers	should	most
decide	as a result	show	some
feel	however	suggest	all
in future	solve	understand	possible

Writing speech

You can make stories interesting when you write what your characters say. This is called *direct speech*. Direct speech makes the story more alive, as if we are listening to the characters speak like they do in a play. There are some special ways of punctuating direct speech.

Example:

The White Cockatoo hopped along the branch and looked down at Dawe. "Hello, Dawe. I see you have been abandoned."

"Yes, I have," replied Dawe. "Why have they left me?"

"The girls are jealous of you. They think the boys don't notice them when you are there. They hope that the boys will think you have drowned, " said the White Cockatoo.

"But I will starve! " said Dawe. "There isn't any water on the island either, and I have finished what I brought with me."

The White cockatoo said, "I have an idea."

"Well," sighed Dawe, "I hope the idea is about water."

Now you try

Think about writing a story that contains a lot of direct speech.

Getting ready

Here are some rules to help you write speech. Look at the example above to see how each of these rules works in a story. ·

Rule 1: You put speech marks at the start and at the finish of the spoken part. *"Yes, I have," replied Dawe.*

Rule 2: There are four ways you can set out the speech:

- Use spoken words only: *"Hello, Dawe. I see you have been abandoned."*

- Put the unspoken words in front of the spoken part: *The White cockatoo said, "I have an idea."*

- Put the unspoken words after the spoken part: *"But I will starve!" said Dawe.*

- Put the unspoken words in the middle of the spoken part: *"Yes, I have," replied Dawe. "Why have they left me?"* (If there are two sentences, use a full stop and capital letter.) *"Well," sighed Dawe, "I hope the idea is about water."* (If there is one sentence, use a comma.)

Rule 3: The spoken words are separated from the rest of the sentence by:

- a comma: *"Yes, I have," replied Dawe.*

- a question mark: *"Why have they left me?"*

- or an exclamation mark: *"But I will starve!" said Dawe.*

Rule 4: A new line is started when a new person speaks.

Steps

Now write your own story using direct speech.

Here are some words you could use

screamed	suggested	told
yelled	laughed	reported
cried	yawned	called out
whispered	groaned	mumbled
shouted	warned	snarled
exclaimed	announced	replied
asked	apologised	sighed
pleaded	repeated	sang

29

Write a traditional story

Traditional stories can be true stories that are part of your family or clan's *history*. Sometimes they are stories that have become myths and legends. *Myths* are stories that our ancestors told, to explain things they did not understand, e.g. earthquakes. *Legends* tell us about the bravery or strength of heroes and heroines who did magical and amazing things in the past.

Example:

The magic pool

Deep in the forest near our village is a rocky stream. There are several deep pools in this rocky stream, but the special one is where the fireflies live.

  Only a few women in the village know where this pool is. They say that if you go there at night, and there are a lot of fireflies, you can look into the water and see your reflection. If you do this, you will become young again.

  One day, an old woman …

Now you try

Write a traditional story that is part of the culture of your area.

Getting ready

Here are some ideas to help you write the story:

• where and when did the story take place?

• who are the characters or people and what are they like?

- what do the characters do and what do they say?

- use words that describe our *senses*.

Steps

1 Write a title for your story.

2 Start by writing *when*, *where* and *who*.

3 Write what happens in the story in time order.

4 Write about the actions of the characters.

5 You can also write what they say in speech.

6 Write what happens at the end of the story.

Some suggestions for a history story are: A great fight against another clan, a great journey that someone went on, a special or frightening event such as a very big earthquake.

Some suggestions for myths are: why something looks the way it does, why some animals are enemies, why some part of the natural landscape looks that way, or is important.

Some suggestions for legends are: a hero in an amazing fight, a hero bravely going on a great journey.

Here are some words you could use

battle	fur	amazing	capture
fight	gift	brave	crawl
body	gold	cunning	escape
cave	head	curious	fight
creature	lizard	greedy	roar
crocodile	monster	huge	search
echo	prize	smoky	turn into stone
face	snake	admire	at last the day came
flood	spider	attack	there lived an old man

Writing a story based on a legend

You can use the traditional stories of your area to write you own stories. You can add more to the story or change the end of the story. You can make the story take place in another time, such as the present, or you can move the story from one place to another.

Example:

The magic pool

"Hurry up," called Gemboe. "If we don't get there soon it will be after midnight and the fire-flies will be gone."

"I don't know why you want to do this, Gemboe. It is only an old legend. That sort of thing should be forgotten now," complained Serah.

The two girls were creeping slowly through the bush towards the magic pool. They hoped they would find out if anyone from the village still went there. The magic pool was supposed to turn old women back into young women, if they could see themselves reflected in the light of the fireflies.

The night was very dark. There were no fireflies on the path. They did not have a torch, only a smoky kerosene lamp that did not give much light.

Suddenly they heard a low moaning noise in the banana trees to the left of the path, in the direction of the magic pool ...

Now you try

Write a story based on a legend.

Getting ready

Here are some ideas to help you write the story:

- Where and when does the story take place?

- Who are the characters or people in the story?

- What are the characters like, what do they do and say?

- Use words that describe our *senses*.

Steps

1. Think of a legend that you could change into your own story.
2. Write a title for your story.
3. Start by writing *when*, *where* and *who*.
4. Write what happens in the story in time order.
5. Write about the actions of the characters.
6. You can also write what they say in speech.
7. Write what happens at the end of the story

Here are some words you could use

the afternoon	a strong wind	poisonous	reached
the bush	a breeze	ghostly	remembered
the climb	my fault	ready	waved
the holidays	the view	afraid	wandered
mangroves	cheerful	awoke	lost (our way)
weekend	cloudy	spoke	lit a fire
cliff	cold	whispered	felt tired
beach	uncomfortable	chased	at night
storm	sudden	crawled	in the dark
accident	narrow	slipped	not far from
cousin	peaceful	hurried	on my way

Writing an imaginary story

An imaginary story is a story that you make up in your own mind. An imaginary story has a *plot*, which tells the reader what happens in the story and why it happens. The plot is often about a conflict or problem that needs to be solved. An imaginary story has *characters* that do the action and say things.

You try

Write an imaginary story with a plot and characters.

Getting ready

Here are some things you need to think about for a short story:

• think of a few *characters*: these are the people in the story

• think of the *setting*: this is the place and the time that the story happens

• think of a *conflict*: this is the problem that is solved in the story

• think about the *action*: this is what the characters do to solve the problem

• think about the *last paragraph*: this tells what happens after the action, and ends the story.

Steps

1 Think of what you could write your story about.

2 Plan the action of your story—what is going to happen?

3 Plan the characters—are they young or old, men or women, what are their names, how many are there, what kind of people are they, what do they look like?

4   Write a title for your story.

5   Write the story in the way it happens—
    start with the first actions and write
    what happens next.

6   Use speech to show what is happening.

Here are some words you could use

adventure	lightning	clear	crawl
basket	market	deeply	creep
beginning	message	easier	disappear
bicycle	mystery	excitedly	explore
brother	passenger	foolish	reach
canoe	pet	frightened	rescue
cemetery	photograph	furious	squeal
cloud	sister	gently	start
dawn	storm	painfully	stop
direction	sunrise	patient	travel
disappearance	sunset	quiet	always
distance	thunder	rapidly	except
enemies	tunnel	serious	inside
evening	valley	shady	outside
footpath	volcano	smoky	all the time
forest	the holidays	suddenly	often
friend	the radio	weakly	opposite
game	accidentally	worst	among
hospital	best	amuse	between
invitation	bravely	arrive	ahead of
island	careless	change	behind

Unit 32

Writing a play—a legend or story we have read

> A play is a story that is acted out, sometimes on a stage, for other people (the audience) to listen to and to watch.

Example:

We set out a play on the page in a special way. Here is an example of part of a play based on a legend called *The Gift of the White Cockatoo*. You can find this story in the book *Legends from Papua New Guinea* and also in *English for Melanesia, Book 1*.

Scene 1. A village close to the sea. Two canoes are on the beach. Several young girls and boys are sitting near the canoes. They are dressed traditionally.

Gia: Soon it will be time for us to go across to the island and get our special shells we use for eating and drinking.

Lapa: Yes. I suppose you, Dawe, think you are too good to go with us and do the work. You think you are so beautiful that all the boys will follow you and help you.

Dawe: *(looking up from the food she is preparing)* You know that only the girls can go to that island. I will work as hard as any of you. Why are you so jealous of me?

Some boys walking past: Oh, Dawe, you are so beautiful. We bet you will bring the most shells.

Lapa: *(speaking quietly to Gia)* See, the boys don't even notice us when Dawe is here. I have an idea. We will leave her on the island and pretend she has drowned, then the boys will look only at us ...

Write a play for your class to act out. You can use a legend or story you have read.

Getting ready

Here are some ideas to help you write your own play.

- find a suitable story that has a beginning, middle and end and some characters

- write about what the scene on the stage will look like

- give your characters names (if they are not named already) and say what kind of people they are

- follow the action of the story so that the characters tell what is happening by speaking or by moving on the stage (you tell the characters what to do inside brackets)

- write what clothes the characters will need to wear

- write anything that you will need on the stage, for example, some cardboard canoes

Steps

1 Decide how many scenes your play will have—call them Scene 1, 2 etc.

2 Write a list of the characters and what they are like.

3 Set out the words the characters say as in the example play.

4 Put comments about how the characters speak or move, in brackets.

Here are some words you could use

cave	gift	trick	search for
stone axe	smell	footprints	lose the way
slippery	knock over	follow	spit
creature	mumble	halfway there	attack

Write a play based on something in your life

In the last unit, you wrote a play based on a legend. However, plays can also be about things that happen in your everyday life.

Example:

The Visit

Scene 1. In a coastal village. There are two houses on the stage, and a fireplace in the middle of the stage. In the background is a painted scene with blue sea, clouds in the sky and some houses on stilts. A woman and a young girl are sitting near the fire. They are preparing the evening meal.

Renagi: Mum, Rachael tells me that there is a letter from Loana. Where is it?

Hannah: On the shelf near the door. Bring it out and read it to me.

Renagi: *(enters house and comes out with letter)*: I hope it's good news. Maybe she is coming for a visit. It's three years now. I want to see my nephew again.

Hannah: Yes, he was a baby when they came here last. Open it.

Renagi: *(opens envelop)*: This letter took nearly six weeks to get here! Any news will be old by now. *(reads)* Dear Mum I will be coming with Kila to visit you at the end of April. Kila is well, and growing fast. I have other news for you too, but I will tell you that when I get there. Love from Loana. *(looks up)*

Hannah: It's nearly the end of April now. Do you think she will stay long?

Rachael: She's coming home! Great! Last time she brought me all sorts of new clothes.

> **Hannah:** I have a bad feeling about her. It's not like her to leave her husband and come home alone.
>
> **Rachael:** We should make a start to get things ready. I like having my big sister around ...

Now you try

Write a play based on something that has happened in your school, home or village.

Getting ready

Here are some ideas to help you write your own play.

- follow the steps for Unit 32.

- think of something interesting that has happened in the every-day life of your family or clan.

Steps

1 Follow the steps for Unit 32.

2 Write the outline of a story. Use the outline to write your play.

Here are some words you could use

music	a choice between	hard work
dancing	the difference between	argument about
fishing	the importance of	fresh air
games	the drums were beating	a lack of
death	in the centre of the village	the reason why
health	a very special time	organise
quietness	in the front of the stage	practice
school	at the back of the stage	speaking angrily
sports	enters the stage	speaking happily

Writer's word list

able	face	light	someone
ago	family	liked	sometime
almost	favourite	living	soon
ask	feel	looking	space
baby	fell	lots	stairs
bad	few	love	start
beautiful	fight	lunch	stop
been	fire	mad	store
being	fish	maybe	story
better	flying	men	sudden
black	food	mouse	sun
blue	funny	must	talk
book	gave	named	teacher
both	getting	new	television
box	girl	night	than
boys	give	nothing	those
brown	great	now	through
buy	hair	open	time
call	half	outside	today
cannot	happened	parent	together
caught	happiness	party	town
city	happy	picked	tree
clothes	hard	place	trip
cold	having	plane	trouble
coming	he's	planet	try
days	head	playing	under
decided	hear	police	until
different	hole	probably	vacation
dinner	hope	rain	walking
doing	hour	read	wasn't
dollars	ice	ride	watch
each	inside	rocket	week
earth	jumped	run	which
end	keep	sadness	wind
enough	kids	same	window
even	killed	sea	wouldn't
everybody	kind	show	yes
everyone	land	sister	yesterday
everything	last	sleep	you're
eyes	later	small	zoo